2016
MODERN WORSHIP SONGS

Produced by
Alfred Music
P.O. Box 10003
Van Nuys, CA 91410-0003
alfred.com

Printed in USA.

ISBN-10: 1-4706-3520-8
ISBN-13: 978-1-4706-3520-6

 Alfred Cares. Contents printed on environmentally responsible paper.

ARTIST INDEX

CONTENTS

EVEN SO COME (COME LORD JESUS)

Moderately bright ♪ = 160 (♩.= 53)

Words and Music by
CHRIS TOMLIN, JASON INGRAM
and JESS CATES

1. All of cre-a - tion, all of the earth make straight a high - way, a
2. Call back the sin - ner, wake up the saint, let ev - 'ry na - tion
3. There will be jus - tice, all will be new. Your name for-ev - er,

path for the Lord;⎫ Je - sus is com - ing
shout out Your fame.⎬
faith - ful and true.⎭

Even So Come (Come Lord Jesus) - 5 - 1

6

8

EVER BE

**Words and Music by
BOBBY STRAND, CHRIS GREELY,
GABRIEL WILSON and KALLEY HEILIGENTHAL**

Slowly ♩ = 69

Oh.

Oh.

Verse:

1. Your love is de-vot-ed like a ring of sol-id gold, Your kind-ness makes us whole.
2. You fa-ther the or-phan,

*Optional: Play cue notes 2nd time.

like a vow that is test-ed, like a cov-en-ant of old.
And You shoul-der our weak-ness, and Your strength be-comes our own.

Chorus:

*Harmony vocals 2nd time.

GOOD GOOD FATHER

Words and Music by
ANTHONY BROWN and PAT BARRETT

20

Good Good Father - 8 - 3

Bridge:
C Em7 Am7
D F♯m7 Bm7
per - fect in all of Your ways. You are per - fect in all of Your ways.
G C Em7
A D F♯m7
You are per - fect in all of Your ways to
D
E
1. 2.
us. You are 3. Oh, this
dim.
Verse 3:
G Gsus G Gsus G
A Asus A Asus A
love so un - de - ni - a - ble I, I can hard - ly speak.
mp

24

Good Good Father - 8 - 7

GREAT ARE YOU LORD

Words and Music by
DAVID LEONARD, JASON INGRAM
and LESLIE JORDAN

Lyrics:
You give life, You are love, You bring light to the darkness. You give hope, You re-store ev-'ry heart that is bro-ken.

Great Are You Lord - 5 - 1

28

HAVE IT ALL

Words and Music by
BRIAN JOHNSON, BUDDY STRAND,
LINDSEY STRAND, MIA FIELDS and JOEL TAYLOR

34

Oh._____   Oh._____

Vamp:

There is no great-er call   than giv-ing You my all.   I lay it all___ down,

*Play cue notes 2nd time.

I lay it all___ down.   There is no great-er love,   no high-er name a-bove.

1.
2.
Bridge:

I lay it all___ down,   I lay it all___ down.___   I lay it all.___   Sing-ing: Oh._____

HOLY SPIRIT

Words and Music by
BRYAN TORWALT and KATIE TORWALT

Moderately slow ♩ = 72

Verses 1 & 3:

1.3. There's noth-ing worth more____ that could ev-er come close.____

**Use cues notes 2nd time *Harmony vocals 2nd time.

Holy Spirit - 7 - 1

40

Chorus:

Ho - ly Spir - it, You are wel - come here. Come flood this place and fill the at - mos - phere. Your glo - ry, God, is what our hearts long for. To be o - ver - come__ by Your pre - sence, Lord.__

IN THE RIVER

Words and Music by
CHRIS QUILALA, JOSHUA SILVERBERG,
MARK ALAN SCHOOLMEESTERS and
RYAN WILLIAMS

In the River - 7 - 1

Verses 2 & 3:

LAMB OF GOD

Words and Music by
ANDI ROZIER, JASON INGRAM
and MEREDITH ANDREWS

*Original recording down 1/2 step in B.

** Optional: Guitar capo 5 in G.

Lamb of God - 5 - 1

2. My name up-on Your heart.   My

shame up-on Your should-ers.   The pow'r of sin un - done.   The

Chorus:

cross for my sal - va - tion.   The Lamb of God in my place.

Your blood poured out, my sin e-rased. It was my death You___ died. I am___

NO LONGER SLAVES

Words and Music by
BRIAN JOHNSON, JOEL CASE, and
JONATHAN DAVID HELSER

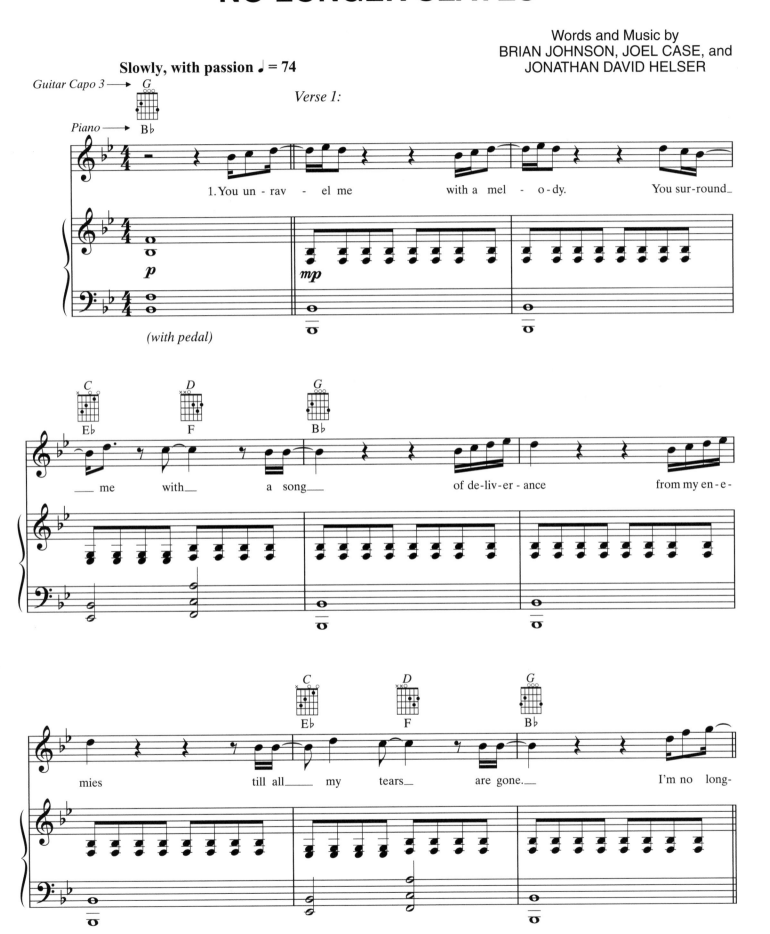

No Longer Slaves - 7 - 1

No Longer Slaves - 7 - 3

58

60

O COME TO THE ALTAR

Words and Music by
CHRIS BROWN, MACK BROCK,
MATTHEW NTLELE, STEVEN FURTICK,
and WADE JOYE

Moderately slow ♪ = 140 (♩. = 46)

Guitar Capo 4 →

Piano →

(with pedal)

Verse:

1. Are you hurt - ing and bro - ken with-in? _____ O - ver-whelmed _____
2. Leave be - hind _____ your re - grets _____ and mis - takes. _____ Come to - day, _____

_____ by the weight _____ of your sin? _____ Je - sus is call - ing.
_____ there's no rea - son to wait. _____ Je - sus is call - ing.

O Come to the Altar - 7 - 1

O Come to the Altar - 7 - 3

66

O PRAISE THE NAME (ANÁSTASIS)

Words and Music by
BENJAMIN HASTINGS, DEAN USSHER
and MARTY SAMPSON

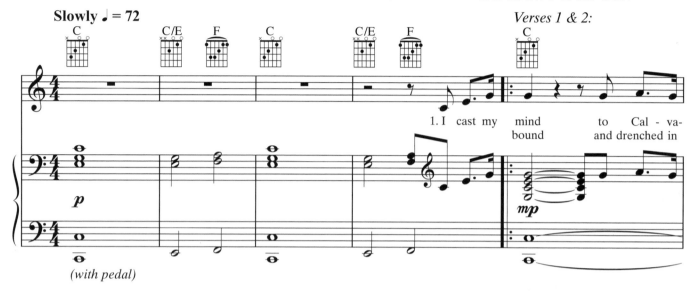

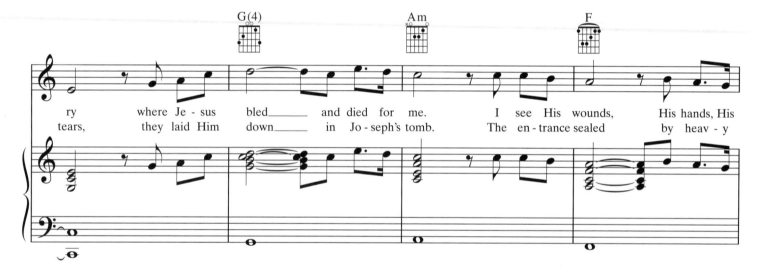

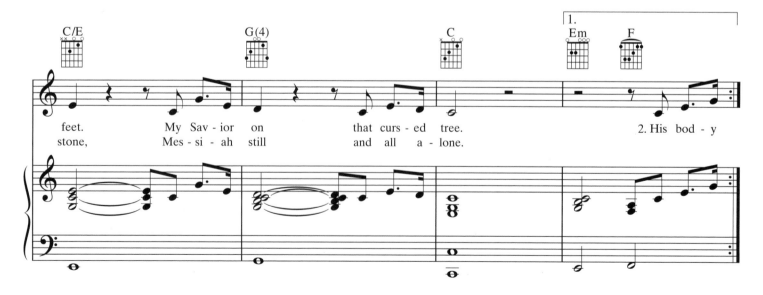

ONE TRUE GOD

Words and Music by
CHRIS TOMLIN, MATT REDMAN and
STEVEN CURTIS CHAPMAN

Moderately ♩ = 96

N.C.

mp

(with pedal)

Verse:

*C

Am7

1. One voice in the dark,____ a song that lights up the stars.____
2. One man on a cross,____ one light of the world.____

**Play cue notes 2nd time.

F2

One breath____ that gives life.____
One name,____ that gives one word.____

* Optional: Guitar capo 5 in G.

One True God - 5 - 2

78

C   Cmaj7/E

the One   a - lone_____ in great - ness,___   the One   who nev -

mf

Am   G   F2   G   *D.S ℅ al Coda*

er chang - es.___   Je - sus,   You are

(Percussion)

⊕ *Coda*

G   Am   F   G

the one true_ God.___   You're the one true_ God._

Am   F   G   C

___   You are the one true_ God._____

REMEMBER

Words and Music by
BRETT YOUNKER, DAVID CROWDER,
JOHAN ASGARDE, MATTIAS FRÂNDÁ,
OLIVER LUNDSTROM and SOLOMON OLDS

RESURRECTING

Words and Music by
CHRIS BROWN, MACK BROCK,
MATTHEW NTLELE, STEVEN FURTICK,
and WADE JOYE

Worship ballad ♩ = 74

1. The head that once was crowned with

thorns is crowned with glo - ry now. The Sav-ior knelt to wash our

88

88

me,_____ yeah._____

4. The tomb where

Verse 4:

sol - diers watched in vain was bor-rowed for three days. His bod - y

there would not re - main. Our God has robbed the_____ grave. Our God has robbed the____

88

THIS IS AMAZING GRACE

Words and Music by
JOSH FARRO, JEREMY RIDDLE
and PHIL WICKHAM

Moderate rock ♩ = 98

1. Who breaks the pow - er___ of sin and dark - ness?___ Whose love is might - y___
2. Who brings our cha - os___ back in - to or - der?___ Who makes the or - phan___

and so much strong - er?___ The King of Glo - ry, the King a - bove all___ Kings.___
a son and daugh - ter?___ The King of Glo - ry, the King of Glo - ry.

This Is Amazing Grace - 7 - 1

92

This Is Amazing Grace - 7 - 2

This Is Amazing Grace - 7 - 3

This Is Amazing Grace - 7 - 5

YOUR LOVE AWAKENS ME

Words and Music by
PHIL WICKHAM and CHRIS QUILALA

*Original recording in Key of B major.

Your Love Awakens Me - 5 - 1

Your Love Awakens Me - 5 - 4

102